A Hat & Scarf Knitter's Pattern Book

32 Project Plans

Index

Item	Project	Receipient	Started	Completed
1				
2				
3				
4				
5				
6				
7				
8				
9				
10				
11				
12				
13				
14				
15				
16				
17				
18				
19				
20				
21				
22				
23				
24				
25				
26				
27				
28				
29				
30				
31				
32				

1

Project ....Item # .... Started ....

Recipient ....Finished ....

Pattern ....From ....

Needles ....Size ....

Materials ....

Fiber .... # of Balls ....

     Oz. Weight: .... Weight name: .... Gauge ....

     Color or Dye Lot .... WPI ....

Fiber .... # of Balls ....

     Oz. Weight: .... Weight name: .... Gauge ....

     Color or Dye Lot .... WPI ....

Fiber .... # of Balls ....

     Oz. Weight: .... Weight name: .... Gauge ....

     Color or Dye Lot .... WPI ....

Notes ....

     ....

     ....

     ....

     ....

Yarn Label and/or Sample Gauge

Photos and Inspiration

Pattern

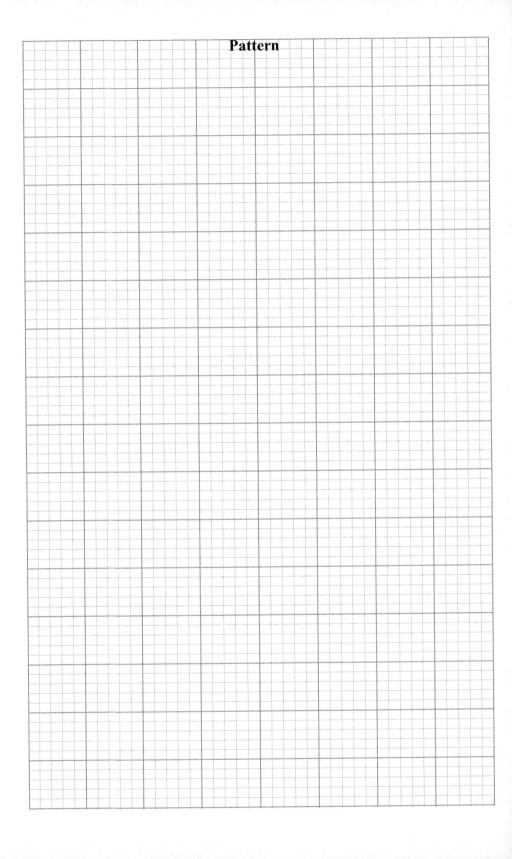

Pattern Notes

Project ....Item # .... Started ....

Recipient ....Finished ....

Pattern ....From ....

Needles ....Size ....

Materials ....

Fiber .... # of Balls ....

     Oz. Weight: .... Weight name: .... Gauge ....

     Color or Dye Lot .... WPI ....

Fiber .... # of Balls ....

     Oz. Weight: .... Weight name: .... Gauge ....

     Color or Dye Lot .... WPI ....

Fiber .... # of Balls ....

     Oz. Weight: .... Weight name: .... Gauge ....

     Color or Dye Lot .... WPI ....

Notes..

     ....

     ....

     ....

     ....

Yarn Label and/or Sample Gauge

Photos and Inspiration

Pattern

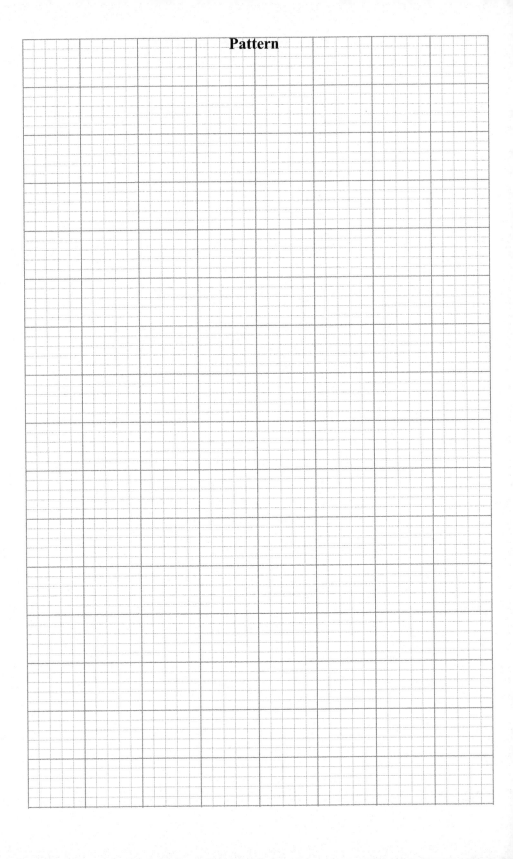

Pattern Notes

Project ....Item # .... Started ....

Recipient ....Finished ....

Pattern ....From ....

Needles ....Size ....

Materials ....

Fiber .... # of Balls ....

     Oz. Weight: .... Weight name: .... Gauge ....

     Color or Dye Lot .... WPI ....

Fiber .... # of Balls ....

     Oz. Weight: .... Weight name: .... Gauge ....

     Color or Dye Lot .... WPI ....

Fiber .... # of Balls ....

     Oz. Weight: .... Weight name: .... Gauge ....

     Color or Dye Lot .... WPI ....

Notes ....

....

....

....

....

Yarn Label and/or Sample Gauge

Photos and Inspiration

Pattern

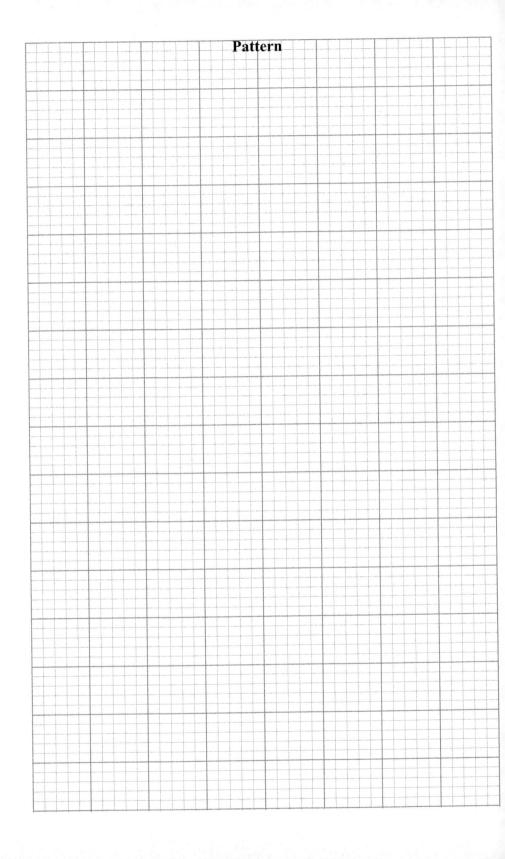

Pattern Notes

4

Project ....Item # .... Started ....

Recipient ....Finished ....

Pattern ....From ....

Needles ....Size ....

Materials ....

Fiber .... # of Balls ....

     Oz. Weight: .... Weight name: .... Gauge ....

     Color or Dye Lot .... WPI ....

Fiber .... # of Balls ....

     Oz. Weight: .... Weight name: .... Gauge ....

     Color or Dye Lot .... WPI ....

Fiber .... # of Balls ....

     Oz. Weight: .... Weight name: .... Gauge ....

     Color or Dye Lot .... WPI ....

Notes ....

....

....

....

....

Yarn Label and/or Sample Gauge

Photos and Inspiration

Pattern

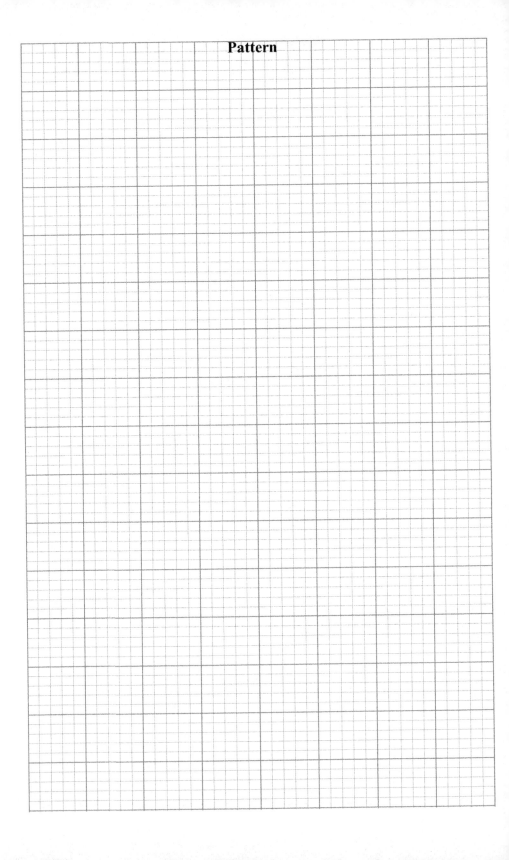

Pattern Notes

5

Project ....Item # .... Started ....

Recipient ....Finished ....

Pattern ....From ....

Needles ....Size ....

Materials ....

Fiber .... # of Balls ....

  Oz. Weight: .... Weight name: .... Gauge ....

  Color or Dye Lot .... WPI ....

Fiber .... # of Balls ....

  Oz. Weight: .... Weight name: .... Gauge ....

  Color or Dye Lot .... WPI ....

Fiber .... # of Balls ....

  Oz. Weight: .... Weight name: .... Gauge ....

  Color or Dye Lot .... WPI ....

Notes...

....

....

....

....

Yarn Label and/or Sample Gauge

Photos and Inspiration

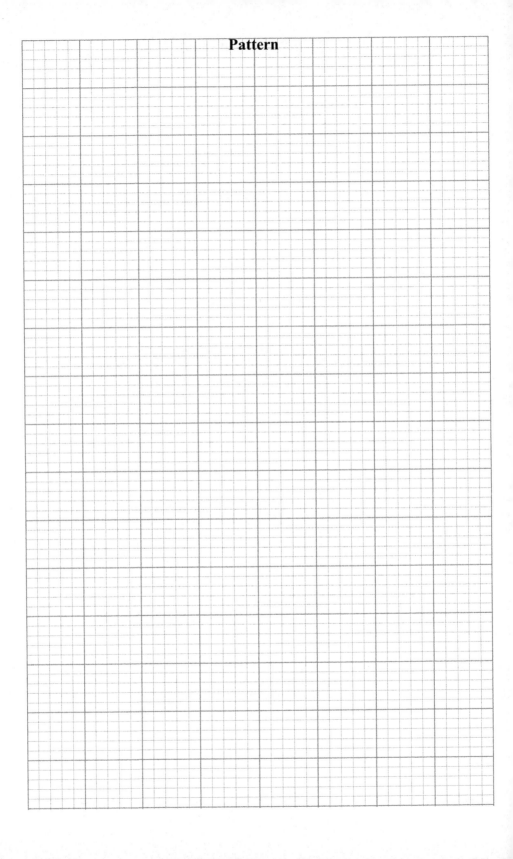

Pattern

Pattern Notes

6

Project ....Item # .... Started ....

Recipient ....Finished ....

Pattern ....From ....

Needles ....Size ....

Materials ....

Fiber ....# of Balls.............................

     Oz. Weight: .... Weight name: .... Gauge ....

     Color or Dye Lot .... WPI ....

Fiber ....# of Balls ....

     Oz. Weight: .... Weight name: .... Gauge ....

     Color or Dye Lot .... WPI ....

Fiber ....# of Balls ....

     Oz. Weight: .... Weight name: .... Gauge ....

     Color or Dye Lot .... WPI ....

Notes...

....

....

....

....

Yarn Label and/or Sample Gauge

Photos and Inspiration

Pattern

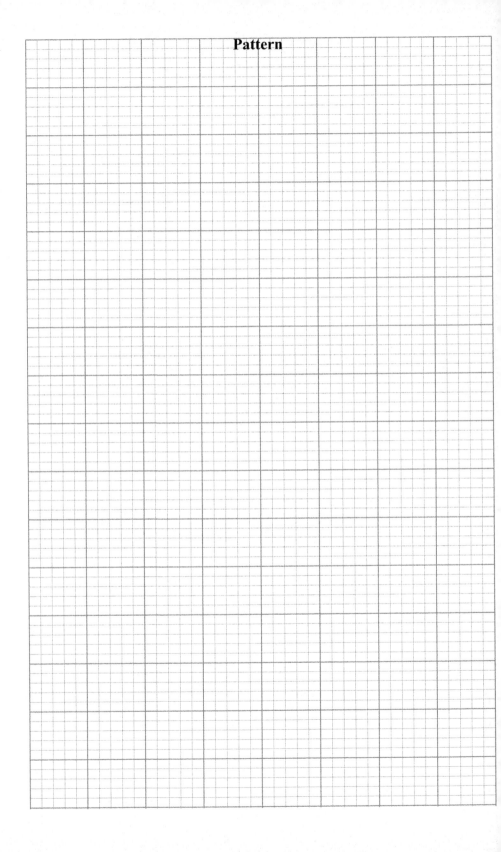

Pattern Notes

7

Project ....Item # .... Started ....

Recipient ....Finished ....

Pattern ....From ....

Needles ....Size ....

Materials ....

Fiber .... # of Balls ....

     Oz. Weight: .... Weight name: .... Gauge ....

     Color or Dye Lot .... WPI ....

Fiber .... # of Balls ....

     Oz. Weight: .... Weight name: .... Gauge ....

     Color or Dye Lot .... WPI ....

Fiber .... # of Balls ....

     Oz. Weight: .... Weight name: .... Gauge ....

     Color or Dye Lot .... WPI ....

Notes ....

....

....

....

....

Yarn Label and/or Sample Gauge

Photos and Inspiration

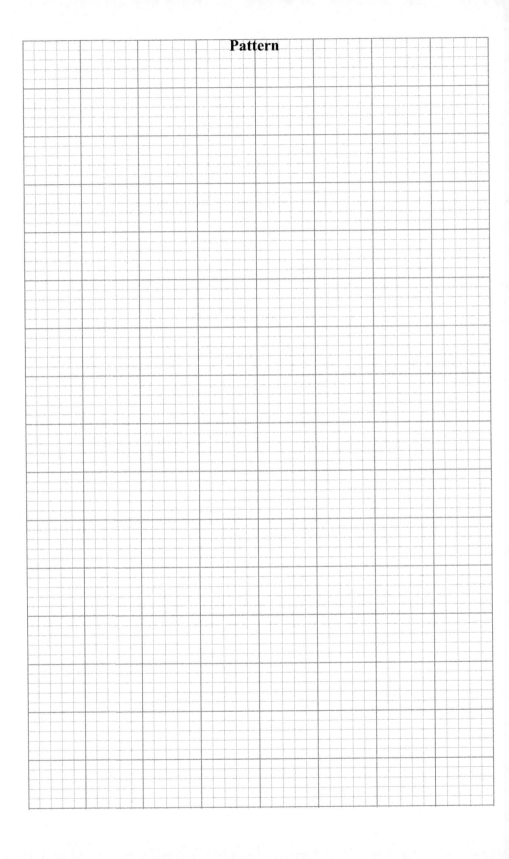

Pattern

Pattern Notes

Project ....Item # .... Started ....

Recipient ....Finished ....

Pattern ....From ....

Needles ....Size ....

Materials ....

Fiber .... # of Balls ....

      Oz. Weight: .... Weight name: .... Gauge ....

      Color or Dye Lot .... WPI ....

Fiber .... # of Balls ....

      Oz. Weight: .... Weight name: .... Gauge ....

      Color or Dye Lot .... WPI ....

Fiber .... # of Balls ....

      Oz. Weight: .... Weight name: .... Gauge ....

      Color or Dye Lot .... WPI ....

Notes ....

....

....

....

....

Yarn Label and/or Sample Gauge

Photos and Inspiration

Pattern

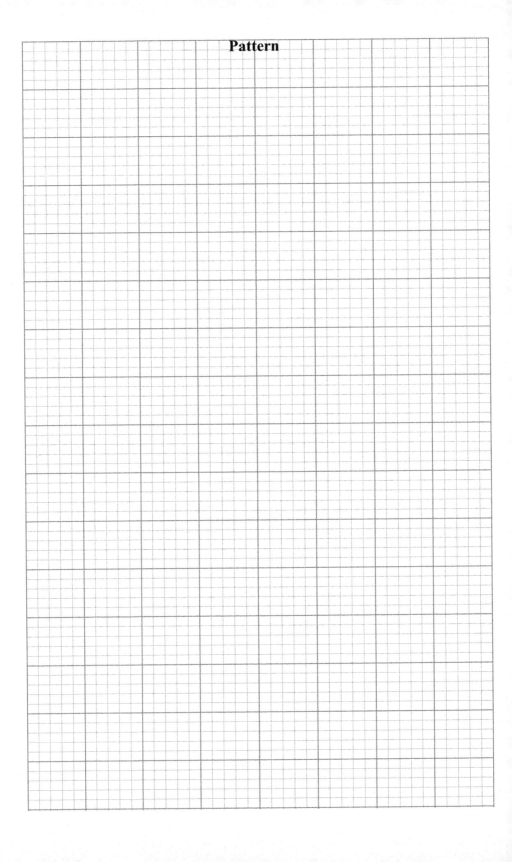

Pattern Notes

9

Project ....Item # .... Started ....

Recipient ....Finished ....

Pattern ....From ....

Needles ....Size ....

Materials ....

Fiber .... # of Balls..................................

     Oz. Weight: .... Weight name: .... Gauge ....

     Color or Dye Lot .... WPI ....

Fiber .... # of Balls ....

     Oz. Weight: .... Weight name: .... Gauge ....

     Color or Dye Lot .... WPI ....

Fiber .... # of Balls ....

     Oz. Weight: .... Weight name: .... Gauge ....

     Color or Dye Lot .... WPI ....

Notes..

....

....

....

....

Yarn Label and/or Sample Gauge

Photos and Inspiration

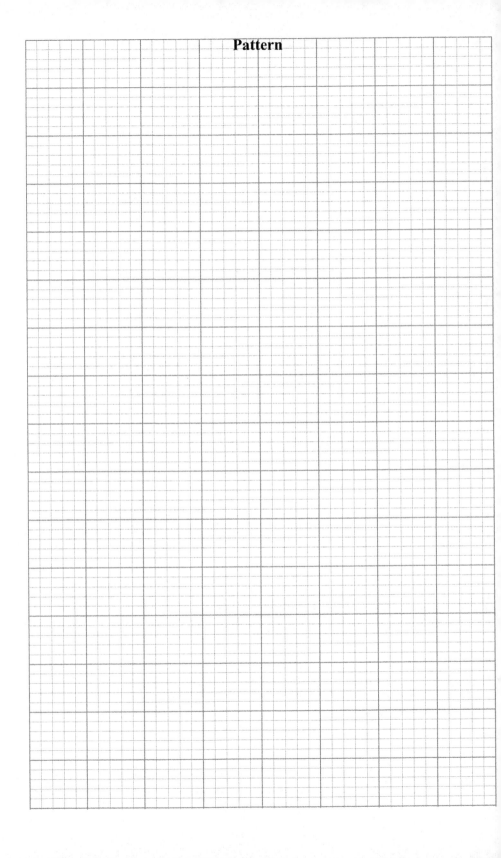

Pattern

Pattern Notes

Project ....Item # .... Started ....

Recipient ....Finished ....

Pattern ....From ....

Needles ....Size ....

Materials ....

Fiber .... # of Balls ....

    Oz. Weight: .... Weight name: .... Gauge ....

    Color or Dye Lot .... WPI ....

Fiber .... # of Balls ....

    Oz. Weight: .... Weight name: .... Gauge ....

    Color or Dye Lot .... WPI ....

Fiber .... # of Balls ....

    Oz. Weight: .... Weight name: .... Gauge ....

    Color or Dye Lot .... WPI ....

Notes ....

....

....

....

....

Yarn Label and/or Sample Gauge

Photos and Inspiration

Pattern

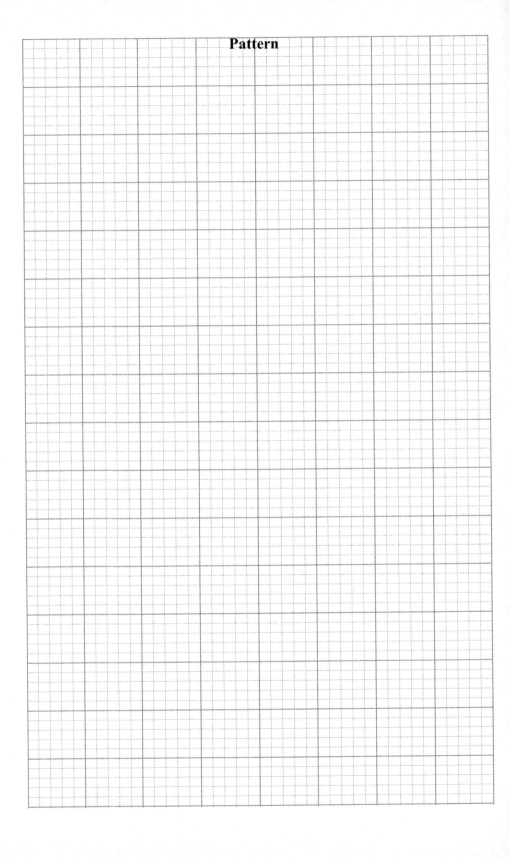

Pattern Notes

Project ....Item # .... Started ....

Recipient ....Finished ....

Pattern ....From ....

Needles ....Size ....

Materials ....

Fiber .... # of Balls ....

      Oz. Weight: .... Weight name: .... Gauge ....

      Color or Dye Lot .... WPI ....

Fiber .... # of Balls ....

      Oz. Weight: .... Weight name: .... Gauge ....

      Color or Dye Lot .... WPI ....

Fiber .... # of Balls ....

      Oz. Weight: .... Weight name: .... Gauge ....

      Color or Dye Lot .... WPI ....

Notes ....

....

....

....

....

Yarn Label and/or Sample Gauge

Photos and Inspiration

Pattern

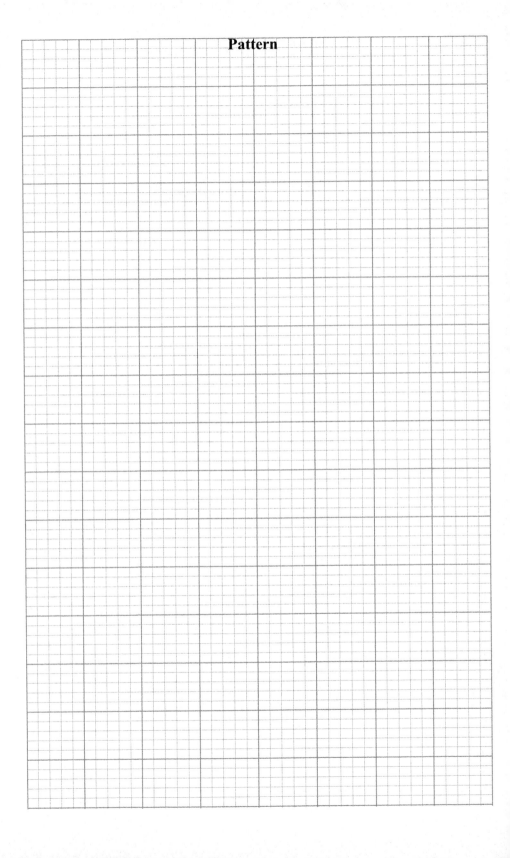

Pattern Notes

Project ....Item # .... Started ....

Recipient ....Finished ....

Pattern ....From ....

Needles ....Size ....

Materials ....

Fiber .... # of Balls...........................

      Oz. Weight: .... Weight name: .... Gauge ....

      Color or Dye Lot .... WPI ....

Fiber .... # of Balls ....

      Oz. Weight: .... Weight name: .... Gauge ....

      Color or Dye Lot .... WPI ....

Fiber .... # of Balls ....

      Oz. Weight: .... Weight name: .... Gauge ....

      Color or Dye Lot .... WPI ....

Notes..

....

....

....

....

Yarn Label and/or Sample Gauge

Photos and Inspiration

Pattern

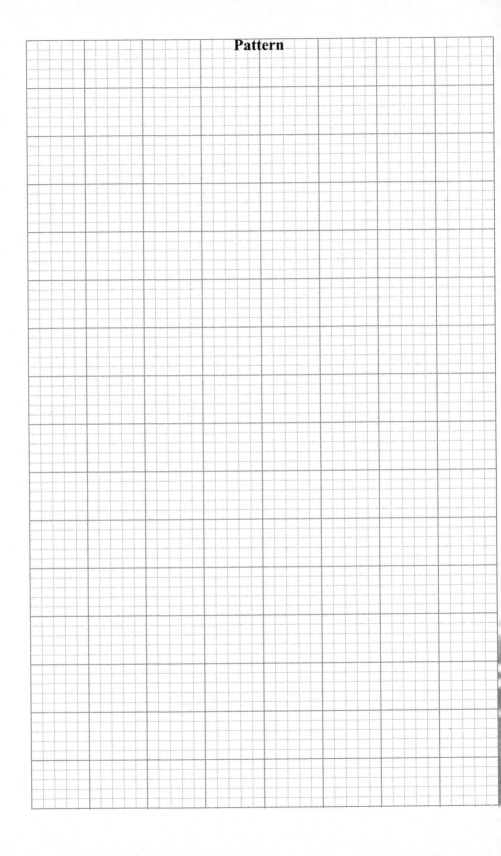

Pattern Notes

Project ....Item # .... Started ....

Recipient ....Finished ....

Pattern ....From ....

Needles ....Size ....

Materials ....

Fiber .... # of Balls ....

     Oz. Weight: .... Weight name: .... Gauge ....

     Color or Dye Lot .... WPI ....

Fiber .... # of Balls ....

     Oz. Weight: .... Weight name: .... Gauge ....

     Color or Dye Lot .... WPI ....

Fiber .... # of Balls ....

     Oz. Weight: .... Weight name: .... Gauge ....

     Color or Dye Lot .... WPI ....

Notes ....

....

....

....

....

Yarn Label and/or Sample Gauge

Photos and Inspiration

Pattern

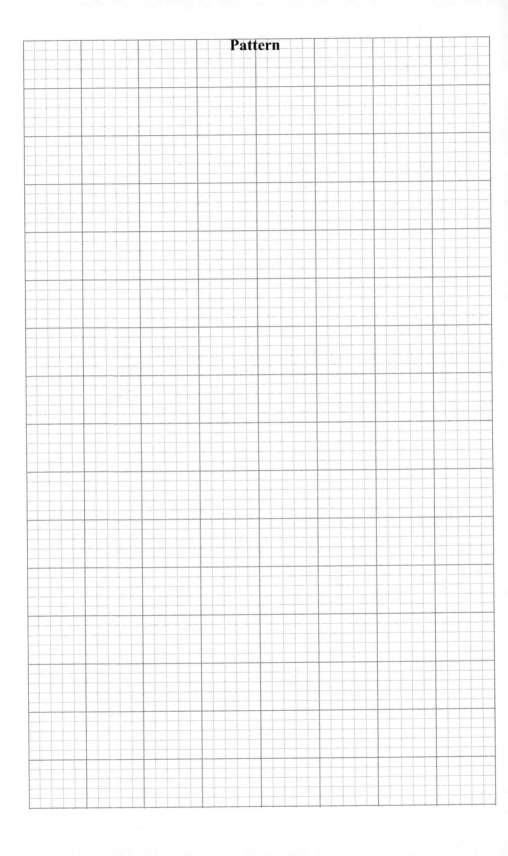

Pattern Notes

Project ....Item # .... Started ....

Recipient ....Finished ....

Pattern ....From ....

Needles ....Size ....

Materials ....

Fiber .... # of Balls ....

      Oz. Weight: .... Weight name: .... Gauge ....

      Color or Dye Lot .... WPI ....

Fiber .... # of Balls ....

      Oz. Weight: .... Weight name: .... Gauge ....

      Color or Dye Lot .... WPI ....

Fiber .... # of Balls ....

      Oz. Weight: .... Weight name: .... Gauge ....

      Color or Dye Lot .... WPI ....

Notes ....

....

....

....

....

Yarn Label and/or Sample Gauge

Photos and Inspiration

Pattern

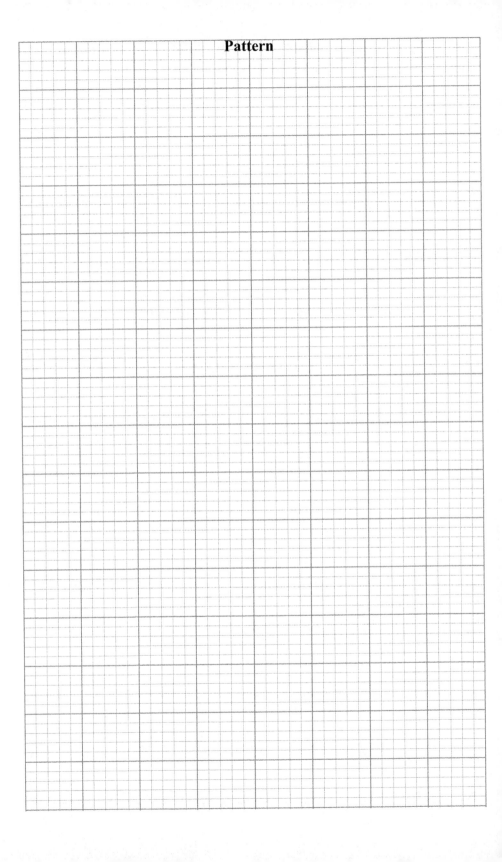

Pattern Notes

Project ....Item # .... Started ....

Recipient ....Finished ....

Pattern ....From ....

Needles ....Size ....

Materials ....

Fiber .... # of Balls ....

      Oz. Weight: .... Weight name: .... Gauge ....

      Color or Dye Lot .... WPI ....

Fiber .... # of Balls ....

      Oz. Weight: .... Weight name: .... Gauge ....

      Color or Dye Lot .... WPI ....

Fiber .... # of Balls ....

      Oz. Weight: .... Weight name: .... Gauge ....

      Color or Dye Lot .... WPI ....

Notes..

....

....

....

....

Yarn Label and/or Sample Gauge

Photos and Inspiration

Pattern

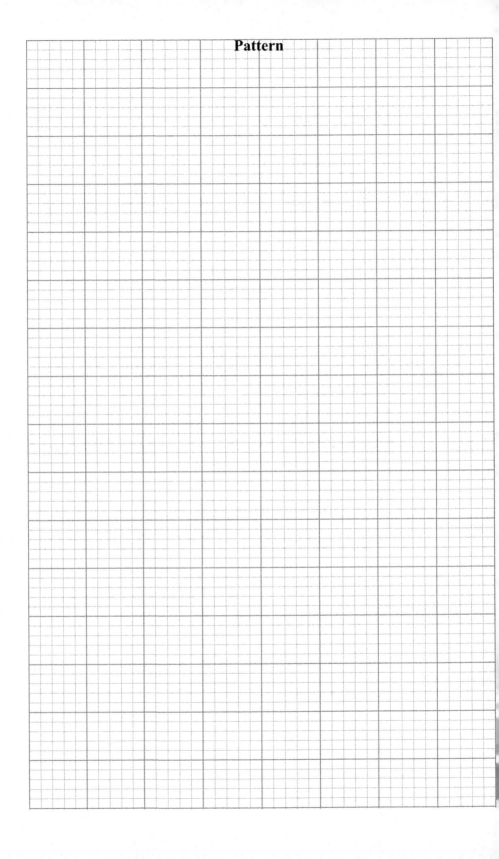

Pattern Notes

Project ....Item # .... Started ....

Recipient ....Finished ....

Pattern ....From ....

Needles ....Size ....

Materials ....

Fiber .... # of Balls...........................

     Oz. Weight: .... Weight name: .... Gauge ....

     Color or Dye Lot .... WPI ....

Fiber .... # of Balls ....

     Oz. Weight: .... Weight name: .... Gauge ....

     Color or Dye Lot .... WPI ....

Fiber .... # of Balls ....

     Oz. Weight: .... Weight name: .... Gauge ....

     Color or Dye Lot .... WPI ....

Notes...

     ....

     ....

     ....

     ....

Yarn Label and/or Sample Gauge

Photos and Inspiration

Pattern

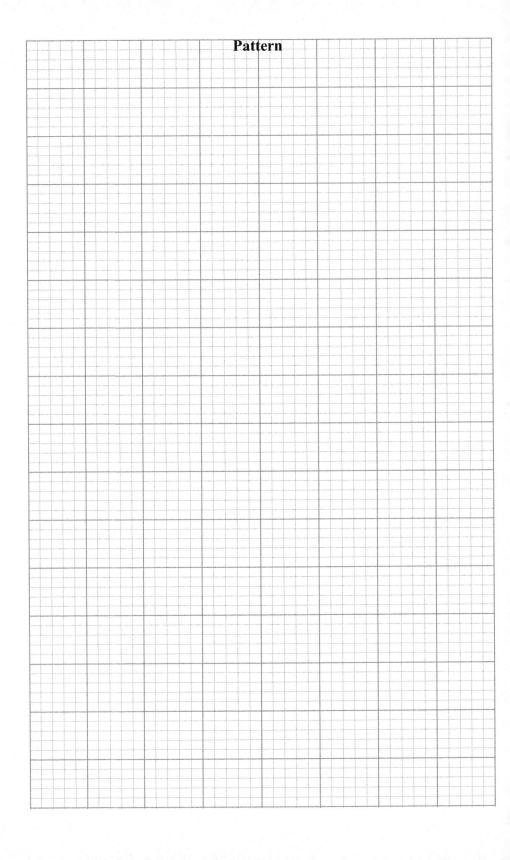

Pattern Notes

Project ....Item # .... Started ....

Recipient ....Finished ....

Pattern ....From ....

Needles ....Size ....

Materials ....

Fiber .... # of Balls ....

     Oz. Weight: .... Weight name: .... Gauge ....

     Color or Dye Lot .... WPI ....

Fiber .... # of Balls ....

     Oz. Weight: .... Weight name: .... Gauge ....

     Color or Dye Lot .... WPI ....

Fiber .... # of Balls ....

     Oz. Weight: .... Weight name: .... Gauge ....

     Color or Dye Lot .... WPI ....

Notes ....

     ....

     ....

     ....

     ....

Yarn Label and/or Sample Gauge

Photos and Inspiration

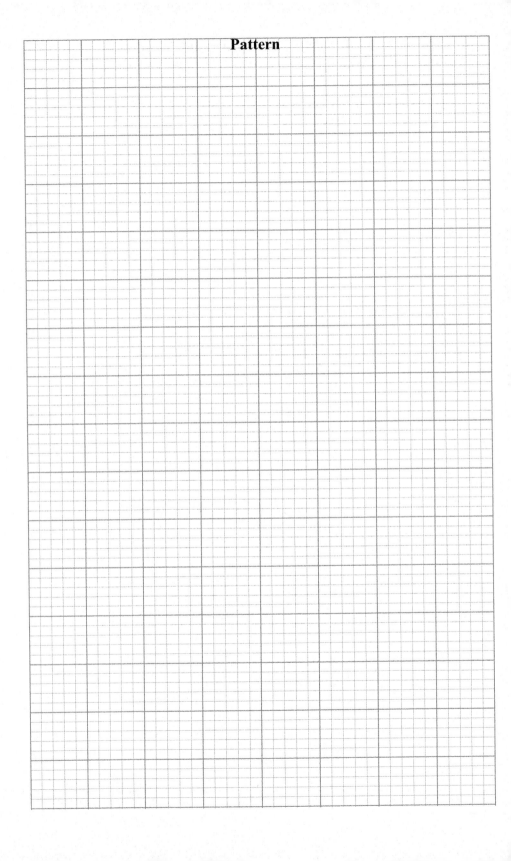

Pattern

Pattern Notes

Project ....Item # .... Started ....

Recipient ....Finished ....

Pattern ....From ....

Needles ....Size ....

Materials ....

Fiber .... # of Balls ....

     Oz. Weight: .... Weight name: .... Gauge ....

     Color or Dye Lot .... WPI ....

Fiber .... # of Balls ....

     Oz. Weight: .... Weight name: .... Gauge ....

     Color or Dye Lot .... WPI ....

Fiber .... # of Balls ....

     Oz. Weight: .... Weight name: .... Gauge ....

     Color or Dye Lot .... WPI ....

Notes ....

....

....

....

....

Yarn Label and/or Sample Gauge

Photos and Inspiration

Pattern

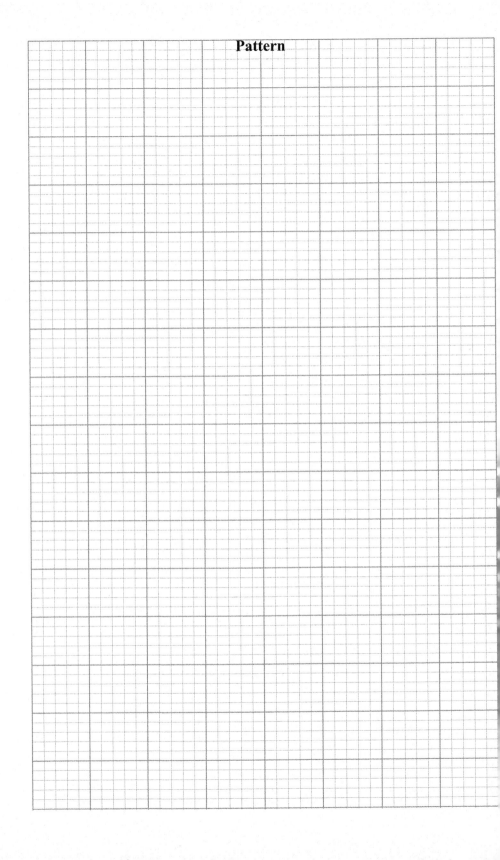

Pattern Notes

Project ....Item # .... Started ....

Recipient ....Finished ....

Pattern ....From ....

Needles ....Size ....

Materials ....

Fiber ....# of Balls ....

      Oz. Weight: .... Weight name: .... Gauge ....

      Color or Dye Lot .... WPI ....

Fiber ....# of Balls ....

      Oz. Weight: .... Weight name: .... Gauge ....

      Color or Dye Lot .... WPI ....

Fiber ....# of Balls ....

      Oz. Weight: .... Weight name: .... Gauge ....

      Color or Dye Lot .... WPI ....

Notes ....

....

....

....

....

Yarn Label and/or Sample Gauge

Photos and Inspiration

Pattern

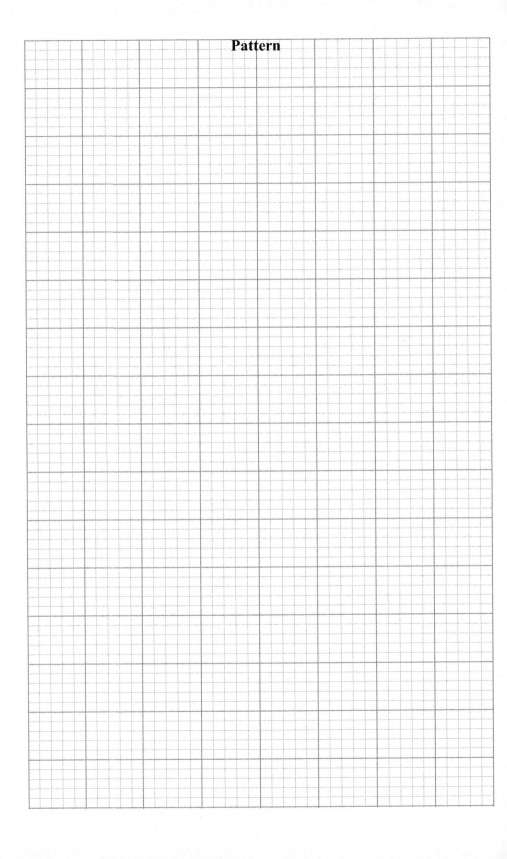

Pattern Notes

Project ....Item # .... Started ....

Recipient ....Finished ....

Pattern ....From ....

Needles ....Size ....

Materials ....

Fiber .... # of Balls ....

    Oz. Weight: .... Weight name: .... Gauge ....

    Color or Dye Lot .... WPI ....

Fiber .... # of Balls ....

    Oz. Weight: .... Weight name: .... Gauge ....

    Color or Dye Lot .... WPI ....

Fiber .... # of Balls ....

    Oz. Weight: .... Weight name: .... Gauge ....

    Color or Dye Lot .... WPI ....

Notes ....

....

....

....

....

Yarn Label and/or Sample Gauge

Photos and Inspiration

Pattern

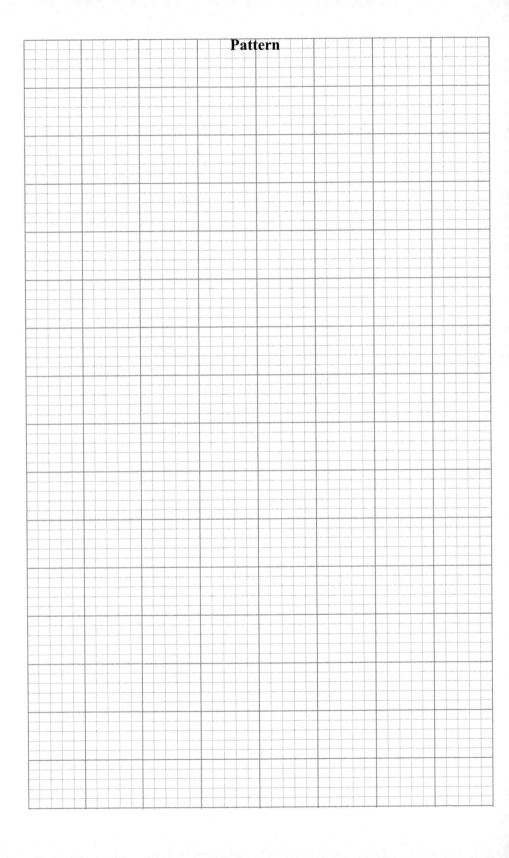

Pattern Notes

Project ....Item # .... Started ....

Recipient ....Finished ....

Pattern ....From ....

Needles ....Size ....

Materials ....

Fiber .... # of Balls ....

    Oz. Weight: .... Weight name: .... Gauge ....

    Color or Dye Lot .... WPI ....

Fiber .... # of Balls ....

    Oz. Weight: .... Weight name: .... Gauge ....

    Color or Dye Lot .... WPI ....

Fiber .... # of Balls ....

    Oz. Weight: .... Weight name: .... Gauge ....

    Color or Dye Lot .... WPI ....

Notes ....

....

....

....

....

Yarn Label and/or Sample Gauge

Photos and Inspiration

Pattern

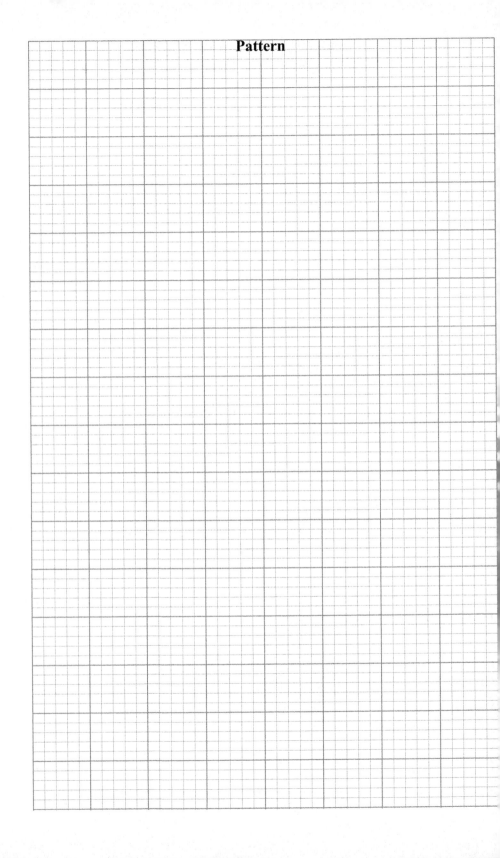

Pattern Notes

Project ....Item # .... Started ....

Recipient ....Finished ....

Pattern ....From ....

Needles ....Size ....

Materials ....

Fiber .... # of Balls ....

     Oz. Weight: .... Weight name: .... Gauge ....

     Color or Dye Lot .... WPI ....

Fiber .... # of Balls ....

     Oz. Weight: .... Weight name: .... Gauge ....

     Color or Dye Lot .... WPI ....

Fiber .... # of Balls ....

     Oz. Weight: .... Weight name: .... Gauge ....

     Color or Dye Lot .... WPI ....

Notes..

....

....

....

....

Yarn Label and/or Sample Gauge

Photos and Inspiration

Pattern

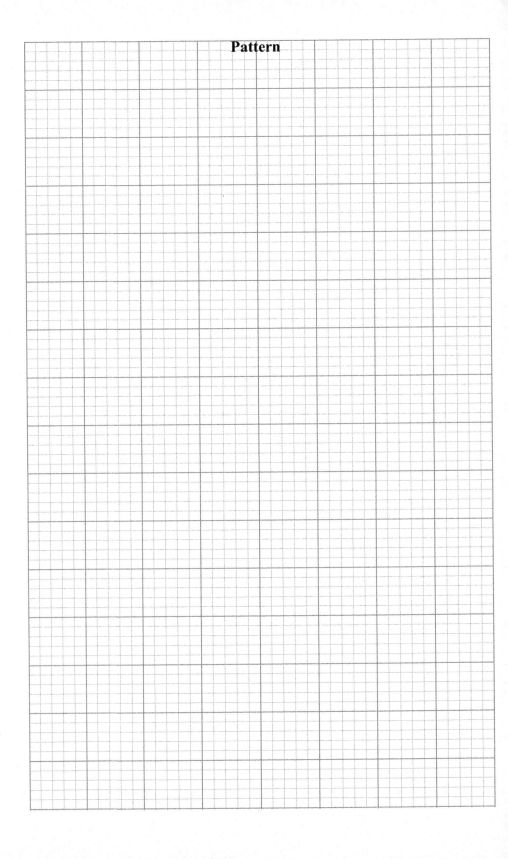

Pattern Notes

Project ....Item # .... Started ....

Recipient ....Finished ....

Pattern ....From ....

Needles ....Size ....

Materials ....

Fiber .... # of Balls ....

      Oz. Weight: .... Weight name: .... Gauge ....

      Color or Dye Lot .... WPI ....

Fiber .... # of Balls ....

      Oz. Weight: .... Weight name: .... Gauge ....

      Color or Dye Lot .... WPI ....

Fiber .... # of Balls ....

      Oz. Weight: .... Weight name: .... Gauge ....

      Color or Dye Lot .... WPI ....

Notes...

....

....

....

....

Yarn Label and/or Sample Gauge

Photos and Inspiration

Pattern

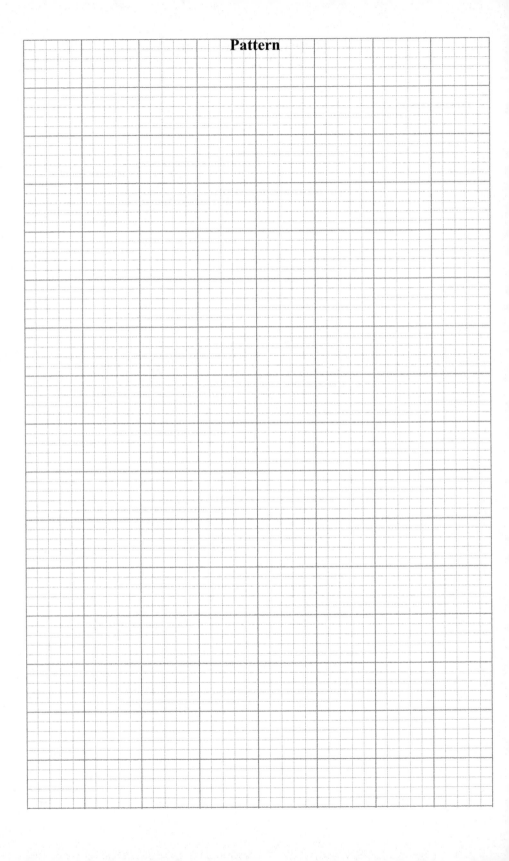

Pattern Notes

Project ....Item # .... Started ....

Recipient ....Finished ....

Pattern ....From ....

Needles ....Size ....

Materials ....

Fiber .... # of Balls.................................

     Oz. Weight: .... Weight name: .... Gauge ....

     Color or Dye Lot .... WPI ....

Fiber .... # of Balls ....

     Oz. Weight: .... Weight name: .... Gauge ....

     Color or Dye Lot .... WPI ....

Fiber .... # of Balls ....

     Oz. Weight: .... Weight name: .... Gauge ....

     Color or Dye Lot .... WPI ....

Notes..

....

....

....

....

Yarn Label and/or Sample Gauge

Photos and Inspiration

Pattern

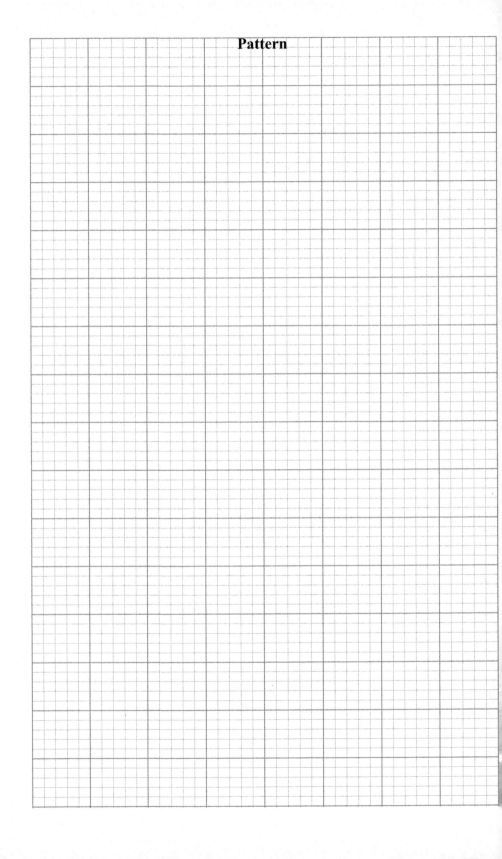

Pattern Notes

Project ....Item # .... Started ....

Recipient ....Finished ....

Pattern ....From ....

Needles ....Size ....

Materials ....

Fiber .... # of Balls...........................

     Oz. Weight: .... Weight name: .... Gauge ....

     Color or Dye Lot .... WPI ....

Fiber .... # of Balls ....

     Oz. Weight: .... Weight name: .... Gauge ....

     Color or Dye Lot .... WPI ....

Fiber .... # of Balls ....

     Oz. Weight: .... Weight name: .... Gauge ....

     Color or Dye Lot .... WPI ....

Notes..

....

....

....

....

Yarn Label and/or Sample Gauge

Photos and Inspiration

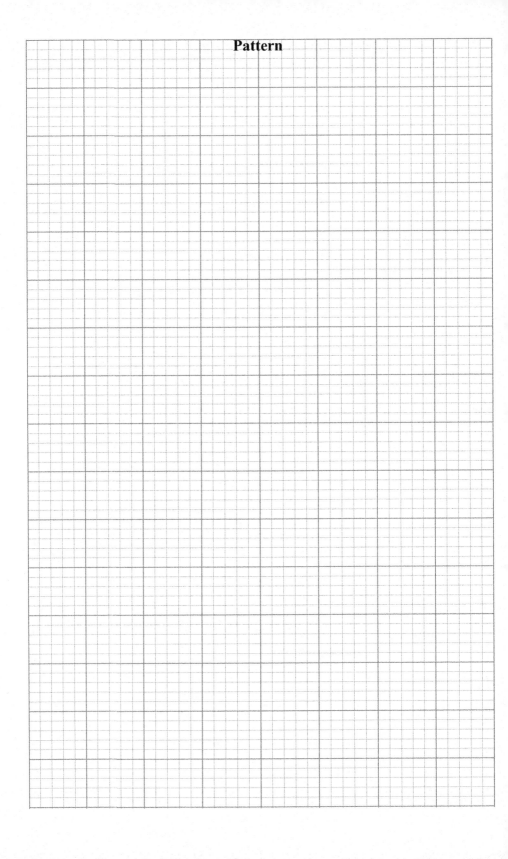

Pattern

Pattern Notes

Project ....Item # .... Started ....

Recipient ....Finished ....

Pattern ....From ....

Needles ....Size ....

Materials ....

Fiber .... # of Balls ....

     Oz. Weight: .... Weight name: .... Gauge ....

     Color or Dye Lot .... WPI ....

Fiber .... # of Balls ....

     Oz. Weight: .... Weight name: .... Gauge ....

     Color or Dye Lot .... WPI ....

Fiber .... # of Balls ....

     Oz. Weight: .... Weight name: .... Gauge ....

     Color or Dye Lot .... WPI ....

Notes..

....

....

....

....

Yarn Label and/or Sample Gauge

Photos and Inspiration

Pattern

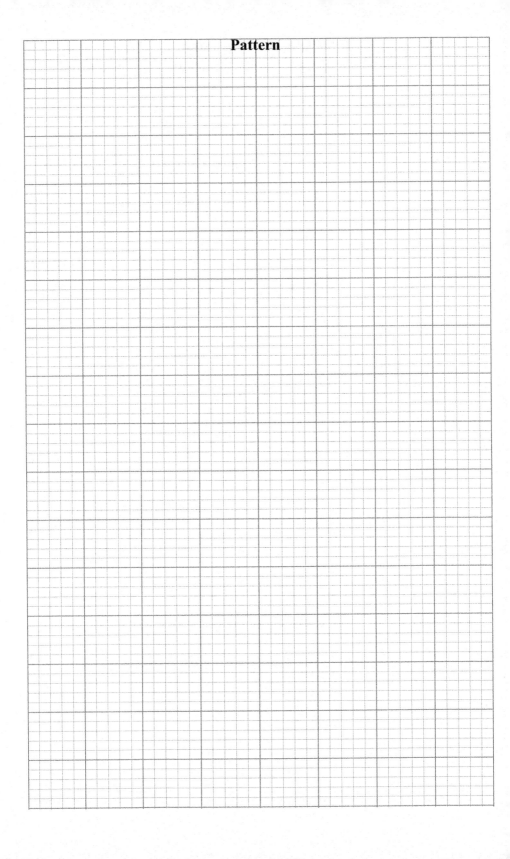

Pattern Notes

Project ....Item # .... Started ....

Recipient ....Finished ....

Pattern ....From ....

Needles ....Size ....

Materials ....

Fiber .... # of Balls ....

    Oz. Weight: .... Weight name: .... Gauge ....

    Color or Dye Lot .... WPI ....

Fiber .... # of Balls ....

    Oz. Weight: .... Weight name: .... Gauge ....

    Color or Dye Lot .... WPI ....

Fiber .... # of Balls ....

    Oz. Weight: .... Weight name: .... Gauge ....

    Color or Dye Lot .... WPI ....

Notes ....

....

....

....

....

Yarn Label and/or Sample Gauge

Photos and Inspiration

Pattern

Pattern Notes

Project ....Item # .... Started ....

Recipient ....Finished ....

Pattern ....From ....

Needles ....Size ....

Materials ....

Fiber .... # of Balls ....

     Oz. Weight: .... Weight name: .... Gauge ....

     Color or Dye Lot .... WPI ....

Fiber .... # of Balls ....

     Oz. Weight: .... Weight name: .... Gauge ....

     Color or Dye Lot .... WPI ....

Fiber .... # of Balls ....

     Oz. Weight: .... Weight name: .... Gauge ....

     Color or Dye Lot .... WPI ....

Notes..

....

....

....

....

Yarn Label and/or Sample Gauge

Photos and Inspiration

Pattern

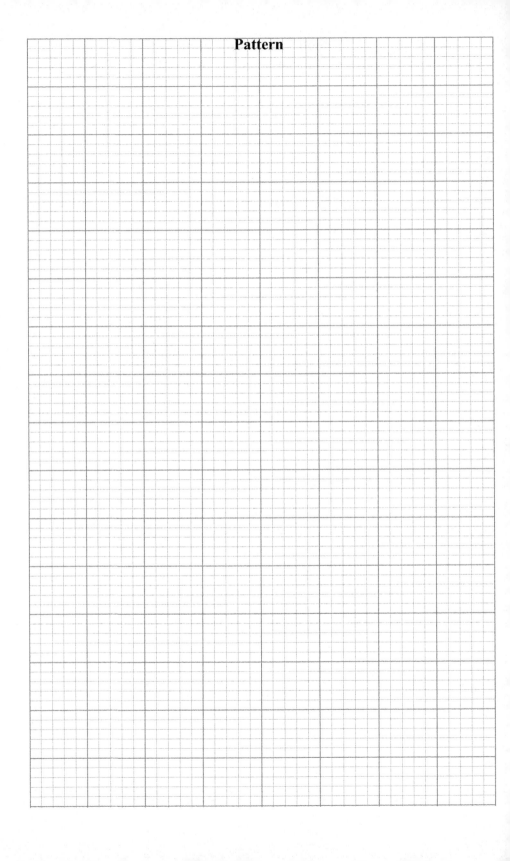

Pattern Notes

Project ....Item # .... Started ....

Recipient ....Finished ....

Pattern ....From ....

Needles ....Size ....

Materials ....

Fiber .... # of Balls...................

     Oz. Weight: .... Weight name: ....Gauge ....

     Color or Dye Lot .... WPI ....

Fiber .... # of Balls ....

     Oz. Weight: .... Weight name: ....Gauge ....

     Color or Dye Lot .... WPI ....

Fiber .... # of Balls ....

     Oz. Weight: .... Weight name: ....Gauge ....

     Color or Dye Lot .... WPI ....

Notes..

....

....

....

....

Yarn Label and/or Sample Gauge

Photos and Inspiration

Pattern

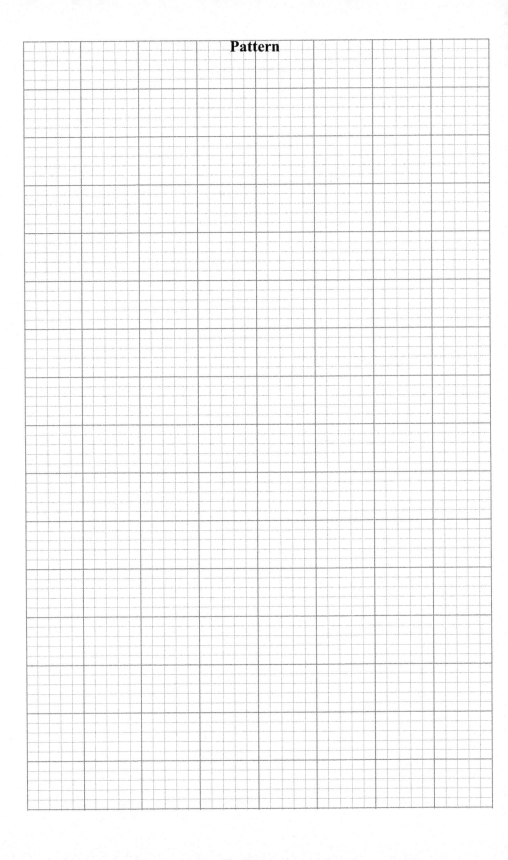

Pattern Notes

Project ....Item # .... Started ....

Recipient ....Finished ....

Pattern ....From ....

Needles ....Size ....

Materials ....

Fiber .... # of Balls ....

     Oz. Weight: .... Weight name: .... Gauge ....

     Color or Dye Lot .... WPI ....

Fiber .... # of Balls ....

     Oz. Weight: .... Weight name: .... Gauge ....

     Color or Dye Lot .... WPI ....

Fiber .... # of Balls ....

     Oz. Weight: .... Weight name: .... Gauge ....

     Color or Dye Lot .... WPI ....

Notes ....

     ....

     ....

     ....

     ....

Yarn Label and/or Sample Gauge

Photos and Inspiration

Pattern

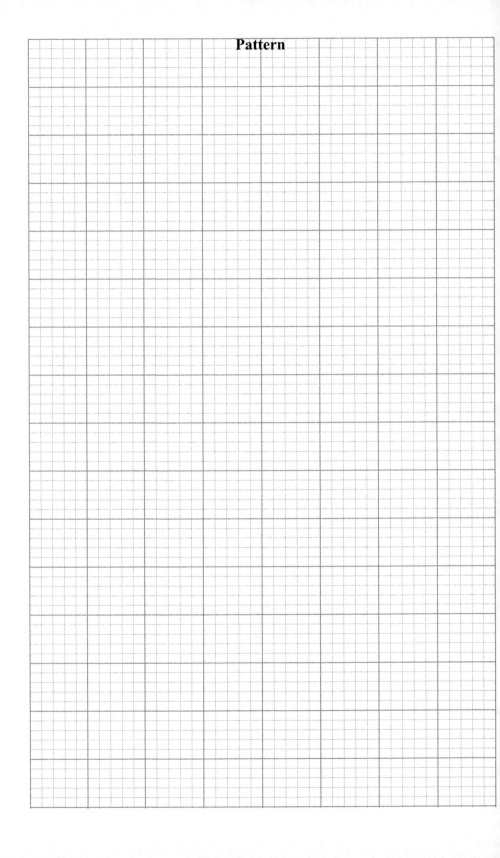

Pattern Notes

Project ....Item # .... Started ....

Recipient ....Finished ....

Pattern ....From ....

Needles ....Size ....

Materials ....

Fiber .... # of Balls ....

     Oz. Weight: .... Weight name: .... Gauge ....

     Color or Dye Lot .... WPI ....

Fiber .... # of Balls ....

     Oz. Weight: .... Weight name: .... Gauge ....

     Color or Dye Lot .... WPI ....

Fiber .... # of Balls ....

     Oz. Weight: .... Weight name: .... Gauge ....

     Color or Dye Lot .... WPI ....

Notes ....

....

....

....

....

Yarn Label and/or Sample Gauge

Photos and Inspiration

Pattern

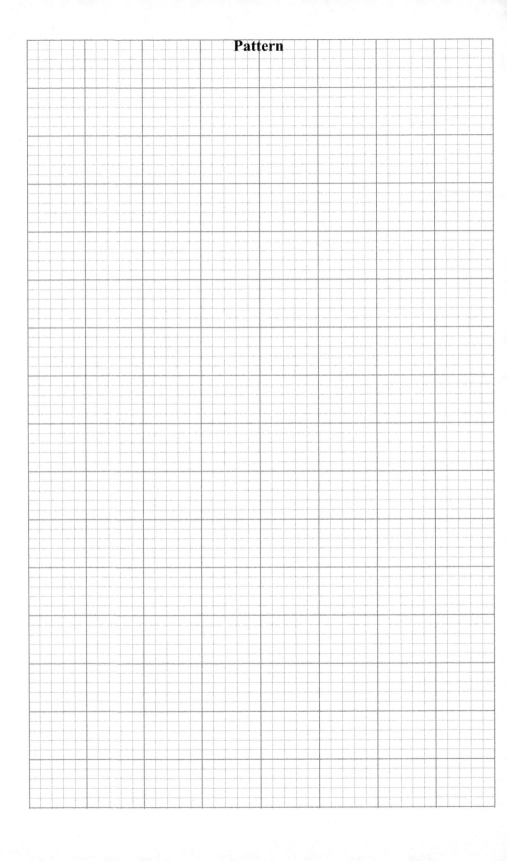

Pattern Notes

Project ....Item # .... Started ....

Recipient ....Finished ....

Pattern ....From ....

Needles ....Size ....

Materials ....

Fiber .... # of Balls ....

     Oz. Weight: .... Weight name: .... Gauge ....

     Color or Dye Lot .... WPI ....

Fiber .... # of Balls ....

     Oz. Weight: .... Weight name: .... Gauge ....

     Color or Dye Lot .... WPI ....

Fiber .... # of Balls ....

     Oz. Weight: .... Weight name: .... Gauge ....

     Color or Dye Lot .... WPI ....

Notes...

     ....

     ....

     ....

     ....

Yarn Label and/or Sample Gauge

Photos and Inspiration

Pattern

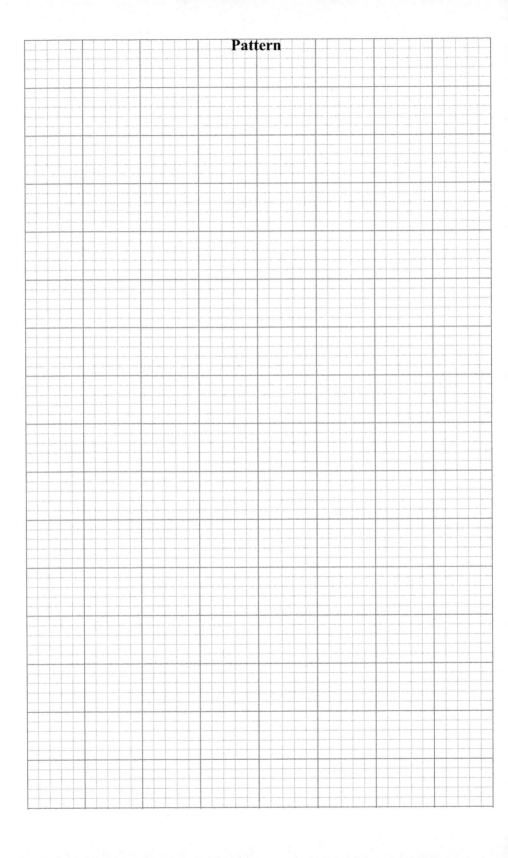

Pattern Notes

Made in the USA
Coppell, TX
16 August 2022